MESSENGERS OF
HOLINESS
Stories of African Missionaries

2016-17 NMI MISSION EDUCATION RESOURCES

BOOKS

MESSENGERS OF HOLINESS
Stories of African Missionaries
by Amy Crofford and Brad Crofford

A MISSIONS MOSAIC
The Changing Landscape in Canada
by Donna Wilson

BRANCHING INTO MISSIONS
Exploring Your Involvement
by Tim Crutcher

AMAZON ADVENTURES
Tales from the Jungle
by Larry Garman

MESSENGERS OF HOLINESS
Stories of African Missionaries

by
Amy Crofford
and
Brad Crofford

Nazarene Missions International

Copyright © 2016
Nazarene Missions International
Church of the Nazarene, Inc.
17001 Prairie Star Parkway
Lenexa, KS 66220
www.nazarenemissions.org

ISBN 978-0-8341-3583-3

Printed in the United States of America

All rights reserved. No part of this publication may be reproduced, stored in a retrieval system, or transmitted in any form or by any means—for example, electronic, photocopy, recording—without the prior written permission of the publisher. The only exception is brief quotations in printed reviews.

Cover design: Juan Fernandez
Interior design: Darryl Bennett

All Scripture quotations not otherwise designated are from the *The Holy Bible, New International Version*® (NIV®). Copyright © 1973, 1978, 1984, 2011 by Biblica, Inc.™ Used by permission. All rights reserved worldwide.

DEDICATION

To Paul and Carolyn Wheelock
and
other retired Nazarene volunteers
who make a difference around the world

ACKNOWLEDGEMENTS:

These resources proved useful as we wrote this book, and we recommend them: Paul Dayhoff's three volumes of African Nazarene biographies, *Living Stones, Standing Stones, and African Mosaic; Out of Africa,* the regional newsletter for the Church of the Nazarene in Africa; *Engage* magazine (engagemagazine.com)—and its editor, Gina Pottenger.

TABLE OF CONTENTS

INTRODUCTION	11
Chapter 1 **SMALL ISLANDS, BIG IMPACT**	15
Chapter 2 **GOD IS GOOD, ALL THE TIME**	27
Chapter 3 **THE NURSE WHO "COULD NEVER BE A NURSE"**	39
Chapter 4 **A FIRE THAT PURIFIES AND SPREADS**	47
Chapter 5 **PARTNERS AND LEADERS**	59
Chapter 6 **HOLINESS IS LOVE IN ACTION**	69
Chapter 7 **A PLACE OF RESPONSIBILITY**	77
Chapter 8 **THE FUTURE OF MISSIONS IN AFRICA**	83
CONCLUSION	89
ACT ON IT	93

ABOUT THE AUTHORS

Amy Crofford is a missionary and writer. She has served in France, Côte d'Ivoire, Benin, Haiti, Kenya, and South Africa. One of her earliest memories is riding home from the post office in a little red wagon after helping to drop off boxes for missionaries. As a child, she read every NMI missions book. She has authored three other NMI missions books for adults and three for children, one with Brad. Amy has also written a middle-grade e-book, *A Rifle for Reed*, available on Kindle about a boy facing difficult choices in 1851.

Brad Crofford is a writer living in the Midwest USA. His articles and book reviews have appeared in numerous publications worldwide. He is a coauthor of *Aunts and Uncles Everywhere,* one of the NMI missions books for children in 2009. As a missionary kid, Brad has lived in France, Côte d'Ivoire, Benin, and Haiti. Brad holds a master's degree in international studies from the University of Oklahoma, USA, and bachelor's degrees from Southern Nazarene University, USA. He is the son of Greg and Amy Crofford.

INTRODUCTION

"We dare not retreat from our calling to spread scriptural holiness. The message of holiness matters! It is transformative, formative, and liberating!" declares Africa Regional Director Filimao Chambo (fi-li-MAH-oh sh-AHM-boh).

What is that message of holiness? Dr. Chambo continues, "God invites all people to enter a covenant relationship with Him, resulting in enablement to respond to His forgiving and sanctifying grace. In Jesus Christ, God has given us everything we need for a godly life. This is amazing grace and love!

"Humans cannot free themselves from sin and its power, but through Christ Jesus, all can experience a new life by participating in God's divine nature. A transformed life is possible in Christ Jesus alone!

"How will people respond to this grace and love without the knowledge of this powerful and liberating truth? People everywhere are in search of a Savior. So often they only know about forgiving grace, but do not know much about grace that transforms or grace that liberates from sin and its oppressive power. The message of full salvation is transformative and formative. It enables people to respond in appropriate ways to God's grace, which enables them to submit to God's leadership for their formation as God's people: people of God, who represent Him in this world. A people who once were not His people but now, because of God's mercy and grace, are godly people—a witness to sanctifying grace.

"Thus, we who are in the light, who are called His people—who are being formed into His likeness—are called to follow Him and be a part of the Lord's redemptive works in this world. This includes participating in spreading scriptural holiness, the knowledge of God and His sanctifying grace for all."

The message must be heard with as little cultural baggage possible, Chambo adds. "The proverb, 'African porridge must be drunk from an African calabash,' tells us that in order for the church to have a bright future, young men and women of Africa need to be fully committed to the Great Commission. African communities need to hear the preaching of salvation and sanctification."

—Wellington Obotte (oh-BOH-tay), Kenyan missionary to the Africa Central Field

Nazarenes of the African continent have never been ones to keep the message of holiness private.

"We thank God for a membership of half a million people in the Church of the Nazarene in Africa. We salute those global missionaries who served sacrificially for the expansion of the church in Africa," wrote Samantha Chambo in *Engage* magazine. "However, most of these numbers were brought into the church by the faithful men and women who loved much because they were forgiven of much (Luke

7:44-47). These men and women believed that being part of the church meant sharing in the mission of Christ."

From early days, Nazarenes of the African continent have fearlessly crossed borders and learned new languages to share the message of Christ with their neighbors near and far. Even when laity move to a new country, they plan to share it.

The Church of the Nazarene was started in many nations by African missionaries who were either working alone or in conjunction with missionaries from other world areas.

General Superintendent Charles H. Strickland wrote in *African Adventure* (1959), "I prayed that the sense of urgency to preach the message of holiness, despite all hindrances, would not be lost—that deserts or mountains or rivers would never deter the *messengers of holiness* whom God has chosen …."

This book reminds us of Africans who were messengers of holiness in Africa and beyond in the past, to celebrate current African missionaries, and to dream with those whom God is calling to missions now.

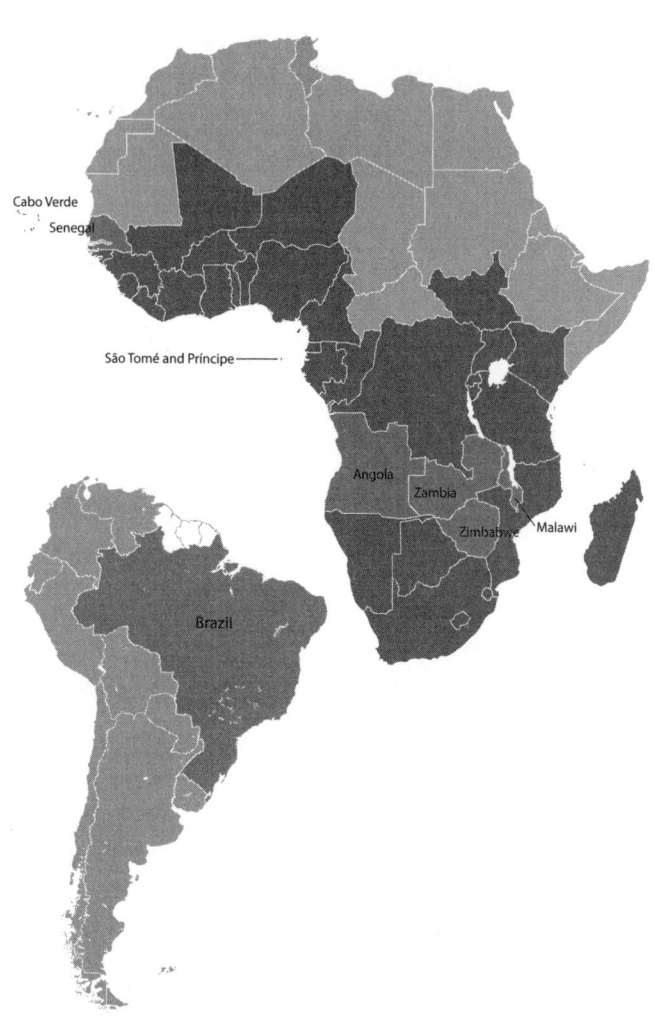

Chapter 1
SMALL ISLANDS, BIG IMPACT

You don't have to be rich to share.
—Benin (BAY-neen) proverb

Pastor João (JAH-oh) José Dias (dee-AHSH) was preaching when he heard the voices. First here. Then there. First quiet. Then louder. And louder. In moments, he realized those in the small mission were surrounded!

"A large mob circled our mission and made so much noise that it was impossible to continue the service," he reported. "The multitude was furious, and we feared they would kill us with clubs, stones, and knives. Twice we called for help from the chief of police. It was almost impossible to restrain the 500 or more attackers."

And this was only during his first year of preaching the holiness message of the Church of the Nazarene.

Pastor João José Dias was the first Nazarene missionary to the islands of Cabo Verde (KAH-boh vair-DAY), then called Cape Verde. Located about 350 miles west of West Africa, these 10 islands in the Atlantic Ocean have a land area of about 1,500 square miles.

A Cabo Verdean, João had sailed to the United States in the late nineteenth century when he was 16 years old. João had been raised in the Roman Catholic Church, but became a Protestant after attending church services in Massachusetts.

At a mission in Rhode Island, João surrendered his life to God, and God called him to carry the gospel back to Cabo Verde. As this young man prepared for his return, he began to testify where he was, bringing his father to Christ and becoming involved in church work.

In February 1901, João Dias set sail for Cabo Verde with a few fellow Christians and a promise of some modest financial support from the Association of Pentecostal Churches of America (which merged with the Church of the Nazarene six years later).

From the outset, the Cabo Verde mission encountered challenges. On their journey, the ship developed a leak, and those on board pumped water for 16 days. Once on land, when João and his helpers preached, they sometimes faced fierce opposition, such as the mob attack he reported during that first year.

In fact, João was frequently roughly handled, stoned, and even beaten into unconsciousness for preaching the gospel. His fellow country members did not understand these beliefs he'd brought back home with him. Even members of his own family spread rumors that he communicated with the devil.

João was imprisoned four times, but even this became an opportunity to witness. Much to others' astonishment, Rev. Dias continually worshipped God and sang songs of praise, like "Happy on the Way"—which is still a favorite for the Cabo Verde church members to sing.

João was not the only one at risk. His followers faced whippings and indignities; abuse inflicted on them resulted with some of them being crippled for life.

But the church remained strong. Even in the face of such persecution and danger, the Cabo Verde congregations grew. By 1916, 87 members were proud to call themselves Nazarenes. By the 1950s, missionaries from Cabo Verde would play an important role in spreading the message of holiness around the world.

Brazilian Boom

A Cabo Verdean man was involved in another country that saw quick, dramatic growth as a result of African Nazarenes' mission endeavors: Brazil.

The first Nazarene missionaries to Brazil, Earl and Gladys Mosteller (mah-STEL-er), arrived there in 1957. Only two years later, the first service for the Church of the Nazarene in Brazil was held during Easter week in 1959, at the home of Elvin Stegmoller (STAYG-moh-ler) a Nazarene who was working for the LeTourneau (loo-TERN-oh)-Westinghouse Company. Nineteen people attended the first meeting, but only weeks later the congregation had grown to forty members.

When the fledgling congregation decided they needed a Portuguese-speaking pastor, they reached out to Pastor Joaquin (joh-ah-KWIN) Lima, a Cabo Verdean living in Buenos Aires with his wife.

By 1961, just two years after the first Nazarene service in Brazil, the country boasted 23 churches and preaching points—three were self-supporting.

Joaquin Lima held a variety of leadership roles in Brazil. From 1968 to 1974, he pastored Central Church of the Nazarene in Campinas, one of the largest Nazarene churches in the world. (It is the largest in membership and the third largest in worship attendance, according to the Church of the Nazarene's Research Services' 2014 statistics.)

For a place as small as Cabo Verde to play such a role in a country as large as Brazil may seem unusual—after all, Brazil's land area is more than 2,000 times bigger. Furthermore in 1960, Brazil's population was over 72 million—more than 340 times that of Cabo Verde!

But, like He did in sending David against a giant or sending the Savior to the small town of Bethlehem, God demonstrated in Brazil that He cares more about faithfulness than size and more about obedience than origin.

East to Africa

Brazil was not the only destination for Cabo Verdean missionaries. The Limas were part of a broader trend.

"In the second half of the twentieth century, a new stage in the history of the church was marked by generations of Cabo Verdeans who left their country not purely motivated by the 'emigration vacation,' but by a heavenly 'vocation,'" says General Superintendent Eugénio Duarte (yew-JEH-ni-oh dwart).

While the Limas were working west across the Atlantic in their ministry, Rev. Gilberto Sabino Évora (sah-BEE-noh AY-vo-rah) and his wife, Clarisse (clah-REES), were called east, as the first Nazarene missionaries to Senegal, then called Dakar (dah-KAR), which was located a few hundred miles away on the mainland of Africa.

Gilberto was saved at a Nazarene church at age 23 and was sanctified at 26. In 1954, while Rev. Évora was still a Bible college student, he went to district assembly. A Nazarene living in Senegal, Mario Lopez, gave him a copy of the New Testament, saying, "Young student, I hope and believe that one day you will use this New Testament in Dakar."

Gilberto pastored in Cabo Verde after Bible college and served as district superintendent for a time, but Senegal would come into his life again through another gift.

In the 1970s, a Cabo Verdean pastor in France gave Rev. Évora a French hymnal. He told Gilberto, "I do believe that someday you will use this book of French songs in your ministry."

Both Mario Lopez and that Cabo Verdean pastor were right.

Years later, at the 1985 General Assembly in Anaheim, California, Gilberto had a vision that inspired him to write this poem:

It had been like a vision.
I saw Africa crying.
I saw Africa affected by severe drought.
I saw Africa suffering.
I saw Africa with its darkness,

Not skin darkness,
Not atmosphere darkness,
But the darkness of the human heart!
However, I also saw God loving Africa and I saw God's hands upon Africa;
And I heard Africans who do not know the Church of the Nazarene, calling for holiness."

After this, Gilberto preached and testified in many African countries, including Burkina Faso (ber-KEE-nah FAH-soh), Chad, Guinea-Bissau (GIN-ee bee-SOU), Mozambique, Senegal, South Africa, and Swaziland. In 1988, he and his family began to study the French language to prepare for their future missionary work. More than 30 years after a man predicted he would use a French New Testament in Dakar, Gilberto Évora was spreading the gospel in Senegal.

The Évoras encountered some harrowing times during their ministry. Once Gilberto was hospitalized and faced a leg amputation. Dr. Nina Gunter assured him that many people around the world were praying for him. God heard those prayers. Gilberto was healed, and the surgery was canceled.

The seeds the Évoras planted are still bringing a harvest today. For example, the first person that he baptized was Antero Fontes (ahn-TER-oh fonts). Rev. Fontes is one of the codirectors of the Institute Théologique Nazaréen/Nazarene Theological Institute (ITN/NTI), which provides theological training to pastors throughout the Africa West and Central fields.

"I learned our mission is not merely to tell people that 'God is love,' but 'God so loved the world,' and we must love one another without racial barriers," Fontes noted when he was baptized. "God loves all people, races, tribes, and nations."

When Gilberto Sabino Évora retired in 1994, he wrote, "There in Senegal, I have my heart, my tears, and my prayers."

From Missionary Supporter to Missionary

While some missionaries, like Gilberto, come to Christ late in life, others are raised in the church and know about missionaries from a young age.

When he was a child, Rev. Daniel Monteiro (mon-TAIR-oh) saw missionaries as heroes because of the way his parents talked about them at the dinner table.

As a youth, he became the president of the ministry group Faith Vigilants, which ran a coffee shop ministry. The ministry was based on the idea that if those involved were going to win Cabo Verde to Christ, they should start with their own city.

When he had been pastoring eight years, Daniel heard a missionary sermon that changed his life. The missionary challenged Cabo Verdeans to realize that spreading the gospel to the rest of Africa was their responsibility.

"To a certain extent, this was something new to me. Together with my wife and church I had promoted the work of the missionary society, challenging brethren to support this work, and even saying that God was calling young people to missionary work. It was just that I never thought this call might also include me," Rev. Monteiro said.

Though he grew up admiring missionaries, Daniel never thought he could be one—yet now God was calling him to be a missionary. He answered the call four years later. In September 1991, he and his wife, Filomena (fi-loh-MEN-ah), were commissioned to go to either São Tomé and Príncipe (SAH-oh toh-MAY and pren-SEE-pay) or Angola.

Not only were the Monteiros Africans who were being sent as missionaries; they were also sent in part by Africans. In November 1991, during the first district assembly in Côte d'Ivoire, attendees gathered an offering to support the Monteiro family.

The Monteiros initially went to Angola in 1992, but they were evacuated when civil war erupted there. Undeterred, they continued to minister, this time in Mozambique, where Daniel became the superintendent of the North District (now the Mozambique Nampula [nahm-PEW-lah] East District). In March 1998, they pioneered the work of the Church of the Nazarene in São Tomé and Príncipe, where they started *A Hora Nazarena*, a radio program designed to proclaim the gospel and to make known the principles of the Church of the Nazarene.

The Monteiros' work carried them across great distances. For example, the capital of Mozambique (Maputo) is 4,706 miles (7,574 kilometers) from the capital of Cabo Verde (Praia [PRIE-ah])—42 miles (68 kilometers) more than the distance between New York City and Moscow. Sometimes it seems like the "ends of the earth" (Acts 1:8) to which God calls us can be on the same continent!

The Highest Levels of Leadership

Besides calling Cabo Verdeans to the "ends of the earth," God has also raised a man from Cabo Verde to the highest levels of denominational leadership. Dr. Eugénio Duarte is not only the first African to serve as a field strategy coordinator and regional director for Africa, but also the first African to serve as a general superintendent.

Eugénio accepted Christ at the age of 12 and was sanctified at 17 after reading Hannah Whitall Smith's *The Christian's Secret of a Happy Life.*

"Lord, I want to leave it all in your hands," he prayed. And God has used his sacrifice!

Eugénio married his wife, Maria Teresa, in 1974 and was elected district superintendent for Cabo Verde in 1987. In 1997, he was appointed as strategy coordinator for the Africa South East Field. A few years later, he was chosen as strategy coordinator of the new Lusophone (LEW-soh-fohn) Field, which included the English-speaking countries of Zimbabwe (zim-BAH-bway), Zambia, and Malawi, as well as the Portuguese-speaking countries of Angola, São Tomé and Príncipe, and Cabo Verde. He also served as the strategy coordinator for the Africa West and the Central Africa fields. He became the director of the Africa Region in 2006.

Dr. Eugénio Duarte

On June 30, 2009, Eugénio was elected as the 37th general superintendent at the General Assembly held in Orlando, Florida, USA. When he was elected, delegates from Africa broke into his favorite song, which is based on a Zimbabwean (zim-BAH-bwayn) folk song and was often sung at the regional office and various events he attended:

If you believe and I believe, and we together pray,
The Holy Spirit will come down,
And Africa will be saved,
And Africa will be saved,
And Africa will be saved;
The Holy Spirit will come down,
And Africa will be saved.

From Cabo Verde to the Ends of the Earth

João José Dias's legacy is a strong one. Within just over a century after he pioneered the work in Cabo Verde in 1901, Nazarenes from those small islands have traveled thousands of miles to share the gospel and have risen to the highest levels of leadership in the global Church of the Nazarene.

A Beninese (be-NI-neez) proverb says, "You don't have to be rich to share."

Cabo Verde may not be opulent in the size of its population, but it is rich in the number of people who have been brought to Christ and discipled because faithful Nazarenes from there shared the gospel, fulfilling Jesus' call to be His witnesses to the ends of the earth.

*But you will receive power
when the Holy Spirit comes on you;
and you will be my witnesses in Jerusalem,
and in all Judea and Samaria,
and to the ends of the earth.*
—Acts 1:8

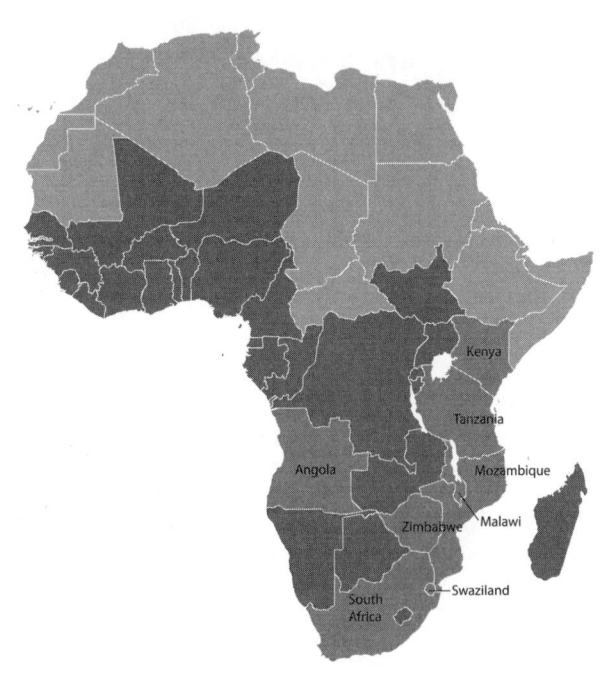

Chapter 2
GOD IS GOOD, ALL THE TIME

Good news is the ears' favorite dish.
—Ghana (GAH-nah) proverb

In productive times, tough times, good times, in-between times, and all the time, Psalm 31:15 affirms, "My times are in your hands."

The truth of this scripture is evident as we see how God has journeyed with African missionaries through varying tempos in their lives.

Productive Times

Less than 20 years ago *Operation World* researchers described the Makhuwa (maw-KEW-ah) as "the largest animistic* unreached people group in Africa, possibly the world."

But they weren't accounting for Jonas and Lousada Mulate (lew-SAH-dah mew-LAH-tay).

A lengthy civil war had devastated Mozambique. Nearly a million people had died from battle or starvation, and five

Animism is the belief that all plants, animals, and objects have spirits.

million people were displaced. But the spiritual hunger and poverty were even more pressing. The Makhuwa and others in northern Mozambique started coming to Christ in droves, especially through the ministry of Jonas and Lousada Mulate, as they quickly planted 20 churches among the Makhuwa.

Jonas Mulate was a train engineer when, in December 1982, God told him, "Mulate, don't drive trains anymore, but drive souls to heaven."

Jonas, son of Pastor Lot Mulate and grandson of Nazarene pioneer Pastor Samuel Mulate, had been sanctified under the preaching of Mozambique missionaries Oscar Stockwell and Armand Doll years earlier. Now, at God's call, he pastored the Church of the Nazarene in the Indian Ocean port city of Maputo while getting his ministerial training. He graduated with a Diploma in Theology degree one Sunday morning and baptized 32 new members that afternoon. During his time as pastor, the church grew from 11 people to 1,200 members.

After having a vision about planting churches, Mulate planted the church in Xai-Xai (shie-shie), the capital of the Gaza Province in southern Mozambique.

Six years later, the southern Mozambican churches sent him to plant the Church of the Nazarene in the northern part of the country. The goal was to start two new districts: the Central District near Beira (BAY-rah) and the Northeast District around Nampula. (These districts are now both included in the Mozambique Sofala Central District.) Although the Mulates were in the same country, this new venture gave them a cross-cultural experience in that they had to learn new languages and cultural differences.

Jonas Mulate sensed urgency in the work. "If we take too long to get to those cities and places that God has given us, the devil is taking over today....We need to work because our time is limited."

The Mulates were not the only Nazarenes at work in northern Mozambique. Many who had been displaced by the war took the gospel with them to places where they settled—whether the new home was permanent or temporary. They built churches with mud walls and thatched roofs. Some had been trained as secretaries and landed government jobs, which proved helpful to the new work both in terms of finances and influence.

The time was right politically in the country. Citizens and others could preach the gospel freely and the harvest was ripe. The Mulates and their colleagues achieved their goal of two districts—and went beyond their vision. By December 1997, the country had 18 districts and 8 pioneer areas with a membership of 35,887.

The church in northern Mozambique was maturing and in good hands.

"God will give us a vision when we forget who we think we are and become who He wants us to be," Jonas wrote. "We must open our eyes, not only to see the harvest but be willing to do what it takes to bring it in."

Lousada Mulate has also expressed her call, saying, "Jesus is my Lord. He saved me, and He fills my heart with His power. My heart is firmly set on the mission to reach the unreached." Jonas remembers, "One night during the preaching at a missions conference for Swaziland and Mozambique, God touched my heart, and I hardly slept that night. I began thinking about all the people in Angola who needed to hear the Word of God. I felt called to be a missionary in Africa, for the people of Angola, and others all over our great continent. The war in Angola is a serious setback, but we have Jesus who is Almighty."

The church next sent the Mulates as missionaries to Angola, after the civil war that had occurred intermittently between 1975 and 2002 wound down. Thankful for the prayers of the members of the greater Church of the Nazarene, he wrote: "As the work is beginning in Angola and São Tomé and Príncipe, one of our top priorities is recognizing and training those new believers who are being called to preach. The journey can be long, and the path can be difficult, but with our prayers and the prayers of brothers and sisters around the world, God is building his church."

The post-war climate in Angola was ready for the gospel, just as Mozambique had been. And the church grew rapidly under Rev. Jonas Mulate's leadership. Eugénio Duarte, field strategy coordinator at the time, congratulated Jonas for his strategy of using the distribution of pamphlets and other printed materials as a first inroad into the community, stating, "From the Namibian border to Lumbango (lyewm-BAHN-goh), Mulate has given away many pieces of literature. People are reading about the Church of the Nazarene and asking about it."

In February 2001, Jonas led a 4,500-kilometre (2,800-mile) road trip from Angola to Maputo, Mozambique. His destination was the Nazarene Seminario (Nazarene Bible college). He and eight students—six from Angola and two from São Tomé and Príncipe—drove through Namibia, Botswana, and South Africa. At a difficult border crossing, Jonas told the future pastors to sing a hymn. The surprised border guard started to sing with them, then stamped their passports and sent them on their way.

At the Seminario, the students attended intensive classes. Rev. Mulate delivered the commencement address December 8, 2002, in the chapel for the five graduates from Angola, two from São Tomé and Príncipe, and several from Mozambique.

And there were definitely places of ministry for these new graduates. The pioneer area in Angola organized after 18 months with 1,100 members, 7 organized churches, and 20 preaching points.

Jonas and Lousada Mulate experienced the truth that God walks with us and guides us during productive times in missionary service.

Tough Times

Being a single missionary has its own set of challenges, as Elizabeth (Bessie) Musimbi (mew-SIM-bee), a Kenyan, can testify. Being single and a woman minister, she faced difficulties breaking through cultural barriers while she served in Tanzania from 1997 to 2003.

And as a missionary, she also dealt with crossing into an unfamiliar culture. The climate, language, and customs were all new to her. As a single woman minister, she faced stigma and resistance. She prayed for God's help and wisdom.

At times she also faced financial difficulties.

"People were looking at me thinking I had a lot of money," Bessie recalls. "Some people believe someone who has come from another country, especially sent by the [Church of the Nazarene] as I was, should be receiving a lot of money."

And of course some of the people she served expected her to share those riches they assumed she had.

Bessie Musimbi

What does a missionary do when she faces such struggles? She turns to the One who ultimately called her. Bessie called out to God for help and wisdom during the dark times.

"There are times when I could cry alone in my room and pray that God could let people understand my ministry," she explains. But she continued to test the faithfulness of God, "I remembered God's command to Joshua in Joshua 1:1–9 to be strong and courageous. I knew that God was with me. God has walked with me all the way throughout my stay in Tanzania. I also remembered God's promise in Jeremiah 29:11, '"For I know the plans I have for you," declares the LORD, "plans to prosper you and not to harm you, plans to give you hope and a future."'"

And Rev. Musimbi enjoyed the good times when she saw evidence of God's hand. For instance, when Bessie showed the JESUS Film, people responded—and many churches were started in the villages where the film was shown.

As she reached new areas, Bessie had to fight some of the same cultural battles over and over again. For instance, after she showed the film in Maasai (MAH-sie) territory, she was to lead follow-up training. She was nervous because despite strong tourism and modern influences, the Maasai still followed their cultural traditions of forbidding women to stand in front of men and teach.

Bessie prayed that God would perform a miracle in the hearts and minds of the leaders so they would listen to her message of holiness.

"The place was so far from the road that we had to ride a bicycle there, which could take us two hours," she recalls. "I was with Pastor Gabriel Chuma (CHEW-mah), the team leader, and Pastor John Mawhera (mah-WAIR-ah). Old men, women, and children were anxiously waiting. As soon as we arrived, they started singing. I was so touched with the response and welcome of these people. We then gathered under a tree. We decided to have a service that day since it was evening. Pastor Chuma introduced me to come and share. When I stood up I didn't believe my eyes as the old men shook their heads, meaning they had accepted me."

Bessie and the film team leaders stayed to lead a week-long seminar arranged around the schedule of the nomadic herder tribe. Bessie taught, but she also learned about the tribe and their many distinctive customs, including their diet, which mainly consists of meat and milk mixed with blood from the animals.

In Tanzania, Bessie also worked through radio ministries. She had a weekly 15-minute program that aired just before the news and a devotional time slot in the mornings. People began to learn about the Church of the Nazarene and its beliefs. Letters from listeners poured in. Many requested prayer. Rev. Musimbi visited those who were hospitalized and prayed with others who showed up at her door.

One man listened to her program with a group of people and came to her to learn more about the church. This small group of radio listeners became a preaching point.

Bessie returned to Kenya after six years. She continued working through the Africa East Field Office. She led East Africa's compassionate ministries for a time. Now she is in charge of Africa East Field Sunday School and Discipleship Ministries International (SDMI). Despite—or perhaps because of—her hard times, her perseverance and passion to proclaim the message of holiness remain strong.

In Between Times

God clearly called Enoch Litswele (EE-nahk lits-WAY-lee) to Zimbabwe. However that's not what the church leaders had in mind; they sent him to Malawi.

Since Litswele knew without a doubt that God had called him to Zimbabwe, he could have rebelled or refused to go. Instead, he chose to trust God in this time between his calling and the actualization of his call.

Litswele was born in 1935 in Mpumalanga (m-PEW-mah-lahn-gah), South Africa. He was five years old when his father left the home. Shortly afterward, his mother died. An aunt took him in and introduced him to the Church of the Nazarene.

Two years after he experienced sanctification in 1952, he accepted a call to ministry. That's when he specifically felt a call to Zimbabwe. Believing education was important, he pursued as much training as he could, finishing a bachelor's degree at the Swaziland Nazarene Bible College (now a part of Southern Africa Nazarene University) in 1960. And in Swaziland was where he met his wife, Ruth, who'd given her heart to Jesus when just a child in the Siteki (STAY-gee) Church of the Nazarene.

In 1963, the church sent the Litsweles to work in Malawi where Enoch learned Chichewa (chi-CHAY-wah) and proved to be a gifted linguist. After one month, he preached for the first time in the new language. "Of course the sermon only lasted five minutes," he later joked.

For two years, he faithfully completed any task assigned to him in Malawi. His message of holiness was wrapped in concepts everyone could understand. For example, one of his illustrations of holiness was, "If a dog is given away or sold to a new owner, it has to be tied for a considerable time or it will run away and return to its old home. The time comes, however, when it can be loosed and it will stay happily in its new home. The freedom to be a happy and faithful Christian comes through freedom from the desire to return to sin."

Enoch's speech has always been picturesque. He stated the purpose of the Bible college in Malawi as: "We are harnessing the power of God's people; as the turbines harness the power of the Zambezi (zam-BEE-zee), so the power within them is directed to God's service. As our graduates minister in our churches, all of our people are better enabled to be the light of the world and share the gospel message of life through Jesus Christ."

While Litswele was serving in Malawi, he faced some health concerns. But there was such a great need in Zimbabwe that the church leaders hesitatingly asked if the Litsweles would be willing to leave Malawi and move to Salisbury (now Harare [hah-RAH-ray]), Zimbabwe.

Dr. Litswele smiled and replied that this was where God had called him to go. They moved and learned yet another language, Shona (SHOH-nah).

After a few years, the Litsweles moved to South Africa for an extended stay. In 1990, they returned to Zimbabwe, this time as officially appointed missionaries, with Enoch serving as the mission director of Zimbabwe.

Dr. Litswele's strategy for building the church involved visiting people, ministering to their needs, and creating a bond so they would see the church as a welcoming place. As relationships grew in the community, so did the church.

All the Time, God Is Good

Productive times, difficult times, and transitional times... most African missionaries face all of these during their terms. But in each tempo of life they can testify that sharing the message of holiness is an experience of learning to depend on God all the time.

Therefore go and make disciples of all nations,
baptizing them in the name of the
Father and of the Son and of the Holy Spirit,
and teaching them to obey everything I have commanded you.
And surely I am with you always, to the very end of the age.
—Matthew 28:19–20

Belize

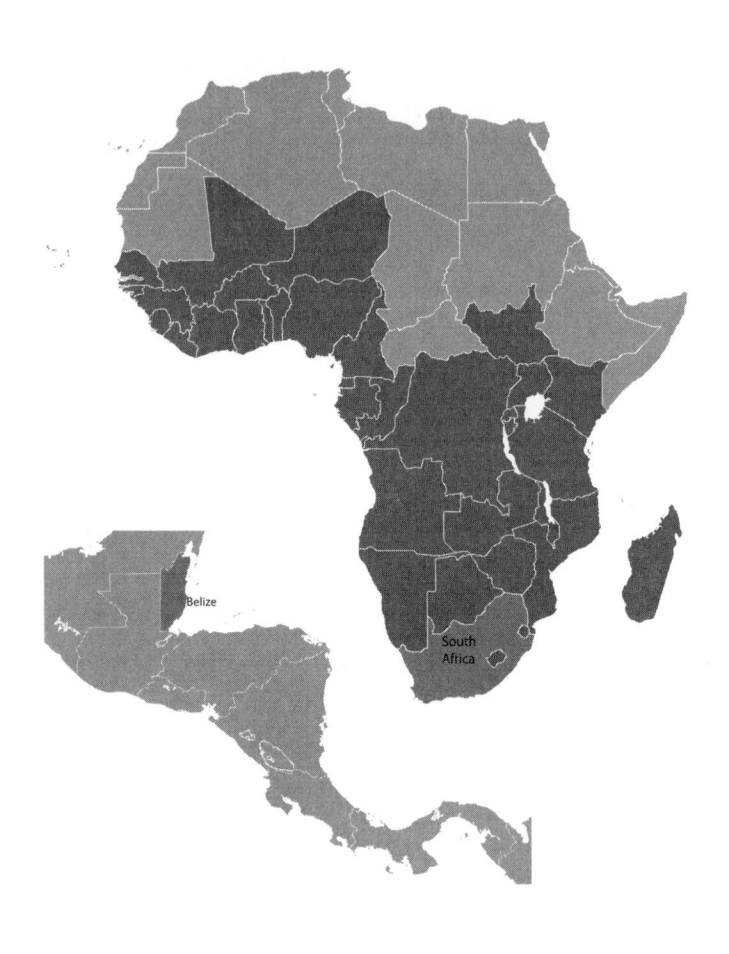

South Africa

Chapter 3
THE NURSE WHO "COULD NEVER BE A NURSE"

One finishes growing, but never learning.
—Benin proverb

Doctors told her she could never be a nurse. She never thought she would be appointed as a missionary overseas. But Constance "Connie" MacKenzie had a calling from God. And, true to that calling, Connie would work for 24 years in that field, including time as a missionary nurse in Belize and South Africa.

An Unlikely Missionary

Born in 1944, Connie grew up in her grandparents' home in the township of Coronationville, near Johannesburg, South Africa. Her grandparents were saved when she was very young, so she was raised in a Nazarene church in Johannesburg.

From a young age, Connie wanted to be a nurse. She was born with a collagen deficiency, though, so every doctor she met discouraged the idea. She told them that if God wanted her to be a nurse, she would be a nurse. She underwent surgery on her knees at age 15.

When she was old enough, Connie underwent four and a half years of nursing training, with a specialty in midwifery. Next she attended Rehoboth Nazarene Bible College (now Nazarene Theological College—in Honeydew, South Africa [serving the South Field]) where she felt God confirming her call to nursing in a dream.

Connie MacKenzie

"I was in some sort of shallow pool, and the Lord was baptizing people in this pool with a crowd of people around it. When Jesus came out of the pool, He gave me bandages and asked me to bandage the legs of the people lying around the pool who needed help," Connie recalls. "I knew nurses use bandages, so He was not asking me to just take care of people generally but to nurse them. I can still see Him coming out of the water with His robes wet and handing me bandages to take care of the sick."

After a year at the Bible college, Connie went to work as a nurse at the Blouberg (BLOW-berg) Nazarene Hospital in northern South Africa. This was a small but very busy clinic, located in the Limpopo Province; and at that time, the clinic's doctor and nurses saw about 80-100 outpatients daily. The Blouberg Hospital is still in operation; however, it is now under the administration of the South African government.

Circumstances on the mission field can be challenging. Both at Blouberg and the later hospitals where she served,

Connie had to fulfill a lot of tasks that nurses would not normally have to do. For example, nurses normally would not pull teeth, but the dentist was many miles away, so Connie accepted that job. She also had to deliver babies—even triplets—that had difficult presentations.

"We had to learn and cope and adapt. Believe me, we prayed a lot. We sometimes prayed those babies out," she says.

Other challenges included problems such as doctors or ambulances being unable to come to the hospital whenever the road flooded. One time, when a river flooded and covered a bridge that a pastor could not see to drive his car across, Connie walked barefoot across the bridge so he could safely follow her.

Was walking across a flooded bridge in front of a car a frightening experience? Yes, but Connie said, "When you are committed and called of God, you do those things to help the people. God has helped me through many things like that."

Sometimes Connie's nursing opened up doors for witnessing.

One time at the remote Blouberg hospital, a drunken man came in with a stab wound he'd received during a fight. Connie discovered that he was holding his intestines in his hand. No doctor was on site, so Connie phoned a doctor. He told her to put the intestine back in, stitch it up, give the man a big shot of penicillin, and send him to a hospital when possible. When Connie tried to follow the doctor's instructions, each time the man coughed, the intestines would pop back out. After another call to the doctor, Connie widened the hole with a scalpel and put in more stitches.

An ambulance finally arrived and he was taken to the hospital, where he pulled through the ordeal. The man returned to the village, and Connie was able to witness to him. He ended up attending a local church.

Belize and Back

While serving at Blouberg Nazarene Hospital, Connie listened to the encouragement of friends and spent a couple of years completing tests and interviews. The Church of the Nazarene sent her as a missionary to the Central America country of Belize in 1976.

This was an important milestone for Connie. She had grown up on a mission district. Could a place where missionaries were at work send missionaries?

Furthermore, this was in the era of apartheid, when people of color didn't get the same opportunities as whites. Could God's call overcome divisive political systems? Yes. Connie was called to missionary work; and in 1976, she was sent as the first dark-skinned missionary from South Africa.

"I never thought I'd go to Belize," Connie reflected. "I never thought I'd be appointed. I never dreamt the church would send me to someplace I'd never been. It was exciting and scary.... It's what God was showing me to do, and He helped me through it."

In 1980, Connie had to leave Belize when the government took over clinics and schools. Still called to missions and nursing, she was reassigned to the Northeast District in South Africa, where she worked at the Thabeng (TAH-bayng) Clinic for eight years.

When Connie's health no longer permitted her to work the grueling schedule and tasks at the clinic, she continued in ministry by working in the Africa Nazarene Literature department and as the field treasurer for the Africa South Field.

At first she couldn't type, but she learned. She couldn't translate between the numerous languages used on the Africa Region, but her significant experience in church leadership positions with young people and missions gave her insights into what the region needed in literature.

Connie had to take a medical retirement in 1993, but she has continued to help as her health permits. God isn't through with Connie!

Called, Equipped, Sent

Connie's story shows that mission work can involve much more than just preaching the gospel, although that is an important part of missions. When she describes what she understands a missionary to be, she talks of someone "reaching out to help people with all their needs, whatever those needs are."

When Jesus sent out the 12 disciples in Luke 9, she points out, He not only told them to "proclaim the kingdom of God," but also "to heal the sick" (v. 2). Our God cares not only about our spiritual needs, but also about our physical needs—and all of our needs!

As people prepare for the mission field, whatever their area of ministry, Connie advises: "Get the best qualifications you can get. Learn as much as you can.... God will open a way for you to get there if you are truly called." She also adds words that reflect her own experience, "You should be very certain of your call, and God will give that confirmation."

So they set out and went from village to village, proclaiming the good news and healing people everywhere.
—Luke 9:6

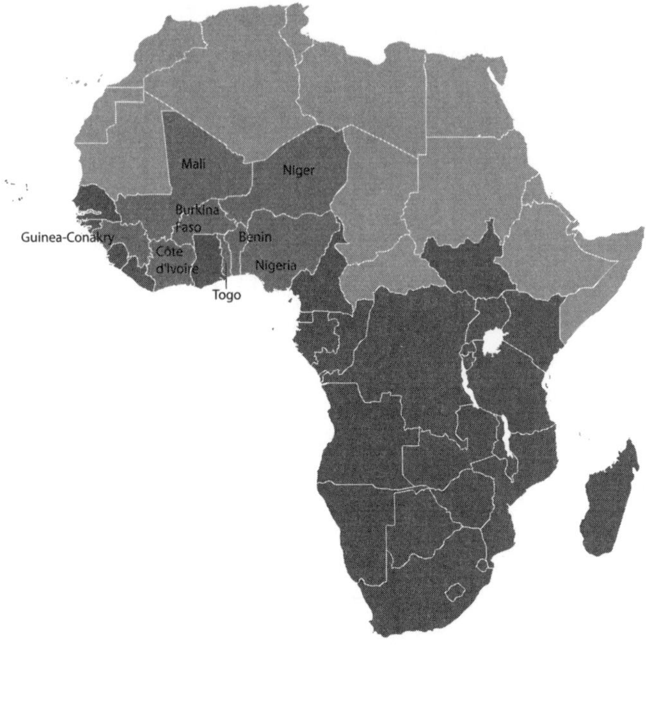
Mali
Niger
Burkina Faso
Guinea-Conakry
Benin
Côte d'Ivoire
Nigeria
Togo

Chapter 4
A FIRE THAT PURIFIES AND SPREADS

When receiving from God, hold out both hands.
—Burundi (Be-REWN-dee) proverb

When God opened a door, Africa West Field leaders did not ask for permission or funding to walk on through and start sharing the message of holiness in new areas. They just moved ahead.

"I am finding that the local churches and districts are sending leaders to other nations or cultural groups where the Church is not yet, to plant the Church," says Filimao Chambo. "These missionaries are supported by their districts and local churches and will often report back to their district at the time of a district assembly."

Carrying the Flame to Conakry

One example of a person who moved ahead is the former district superintendent of Côte d'Ivoire and current area coordinator of Burkina Faso, Guinea Conakry* (GIN-

---

*Guinea Conakry is a world area in West Africa, formerly known as French Guinea, and also known as Guinea. When the Church of the Nazarene entered it in 2009, the decision was made to refer to it as "Guinea Conakry."

ee KAH-nah-kree), and Mali (MAH-lee), Clément Djédjé (KLAY-maunt JAY-JAY).

Dr. Chambo notes that Djédjé is an example of a person who moved ahead from the beginning of his work in the Church of the Nazarene. "The fact that we were not able to deploy Djédjé as a missionary did not stop him from beginning to follow and obey God's call in his life."

In early 2008, the Andokoi (ahn-doh-KWAH) Church in southern Côte d'Ivoire asked then District Superintendent Clément Djédjé to bring the Church of the Nazarene to their home country. Clément had already proven his heart for missions by teaching classes in Benin and developing a close mentoring relationship with Möise Toumoudagou (moh-EEZ tew-mew-DAH-gew). Although Djédjé is no longer a young man, the fire in him burns strong. He accepted the challenge to begin the work in a new country where religious practitioners are 85 percent Muslim, 8 percent Christian, and 7 percent traditional African religion.

In March, Djédjé climbed in his car and headed northwest in temperatures nearing 35°C (95°F). The drive would take about 10 hours, not including time for the border crossing. This was not an easy trip. He got stuck in the mud and crossed a homemade stick bridge over a stream. Yet, he continued. His destination was the provincial capital of eastern Guinea Conakry, N'Zélékoré (zay-lay-KOR-ay).

Djédjé had been a French teacher for many years before becoming a pastor and teacher at the Institut Théologique Nazaréen (Nazarene Theological Institute). He used his language ability on this first trip to this neighboring French-speaking nation. The people accepted the passionate presentation of holiness evangelism. At the end of the week of leadership and membership training, 30 people joined the church and a local congregation began. By February 2009, the Central Church in N'Zérékoré had 150 members and six cell groups.

At the General Board meeting later in 2009, permission was given to begin the work in Guinea Conakry. The fire of the Spirit goes where it will, when it will.

Clément & Lucie Djédjé

God works through JESUS Film presentations. In Guinea Conakry, a woman reported having nightmares such that she had no rest, yet the instant she accepted Christ, she felt freed from all evil. That night she slept peacefully. Many people who were converted brought their fetishes, inanimate objects worshiped for supposed magical powers, to be burned publicly. Praise God for a fire that not only spreads, but also purifies.

In another village, 135 people accepted Christ over two days. After the Sunday service, 50 were baptized. People were healed and delivered from demons. Three men brought their fetishes to be burned.

What message caught the people's imagination? In Djédjé's book, *Sorcéllerie et Saintété* ([soh-sel-e-REE ay sahn-tay-TAY] *Witchcraft and Holiness*), he wrote:

> We are fully convinced that the sorcerer has no power over a child of God, even if he does not hesitate to attack often. The sanctified Christian does not fear the fiery darts of the devil because he or she walks through the Holy Spirit whose power is above all power.
>
> The wizards do not fear Christian verbiage. What they fear is Christ Himself. And He lives in us; witchcraft loses its power over us....
>
> We want to demonstrate the omnipotence of God's Spirit on any other spirit. African Nazarenes have no reason to continue to live in fear and the fear of witchcraft. They have no reason to be swayed by the stories of mystical powers and criminal sorcerers. A holy Christian has nothing to fear from these predators of the world of darkness. Jesus defeated sin. Jesus has overcome the world. Jesus defeated the devil. What would we fear?

As Guinea Conakry's Nazarene movement grew, the first elder was ordained in November 2013.

In 2015, the Africa Region appointed Clément Djédjé as an official regional missionary. His assignment is area coordinator of Burkina Faso, Guinea Conakry, and Mali. He and his wife, Lucie, have moved to Mali where they will doubtless spread a new fire for Christ.

First Assembly, First Missionary Sent

"God does not have a program of mission, God *is* mission," says Dr. David Wesley, professor of missions at Nazarene Theological Seminary, USA. "The body of Christ, therefore, shares that image of God. The church in Benin was not waiting for outside money or approval. They were just doing what is natural for the body of Christ, just as the church in the first century did. They live as a Christian witness in their own community, but also look outward to areas with little or no Christian witness."

In northern Benin, laypeople of all ages take the message of holiness to their own people and the places they know, resulting in quick church growth. They accept the challenge to use their family and personal and professional contacts as channels for evangelism. They do not limit themselves to a local vision, but also see their neighbors as needing Christ.

At the first Benin Pendjari (pend-JAR-ee) District Assembly, leaders of the meeting asked for someone to serve as a volunteer missionary to the unreached northern area of Togo, with whom they share a border.

Pastor Apolli (ah-POH-li) raised his hand.

Officially, this Beninese district was only one year old, but it started with 400 organized churches. As the result of miraculous church growth, the district that had covered

Benin and Togo split into five districts, and the Benin Pendjari District was one of them.

When it was determined that Pastor Apolli and his family would go, those attending the assembly acted immediately. They took an offering to provide transportation for the Apolli family. The women's ministry gathered enough food to feed the family for a month. The JESUS Film Harvest Partners ministry gave him a backpack with equipment to show the film.

So Apolli and his family began the journey of spreading the message of holiness to a new area. He did not know how he would earn a living, where they would live, or any other details about the future. He trusted God with what he did not know as well as with what he did know. He did know that the area was intensely animistic. The people live in fear of evil spirits and worship idols. Their beliefs are a mix of many religious traditions.

The Togolese (toh-goh-LEES) proved ready and open to hear about the gospel and holiness. Within six months, Apolli had planted 23 churches. The new Nazarenes wanted him to be free to travel with this life-changing message. They gave him and his family a place to live and food to eat. They also gave him a bicycle so he could visit villages even further away.

Truly the fire of the Holy Spirit burned in their hearts, and it would not be put out.

The Burning Desert

The Sahel (sah-HEL) Initiative of the Africa West Field is a coordinated effort to spread the message of holiness across the long-established trade route hedging the southern edge of the Sahara. The work in both Niger (nie-JER) and Mali has resulted from local leaders crossing borders and planting churches where God's Spirit moves them.

A leader from Benin explains, "Five districts share a border with Niger, and we felt this area needed a mission or mission presence. So when [we] strategized about the Sahel movement initiative, we identified people groups who live along the border of Benin and Niger. Many had never heard the gospel. People in our churches saw the need of those people, and we decided to send a missionary."

The missionary who was sent has the necessary skills and commitment to be effective in this setting. Lives have been changed. The sick have been healed.

Why Abuja (ah-BEW-jah)?

The message of holiness often is known in one part of a country and unheard of in others.

The history of the Church of the Nazarene in Nigeria is unique. A Nazarene serviceman who was in the Eastern Hemisphere during World War II met a Nigerian soldier. The Nigerian was impressed by the Nazarene beliefs; and after returning to his home country, he wrote to the Church of the Nazarene's administrative offices to request more information about the denomination. Whoever received his letter sent him the *Manual.* He read the book, and then he and some friends registered the church with the government in 1946 and began holding services in the rural southeast corner of the country.

Later, when the Africa West Field was organized and the leaders took a scouting trip to Nigeria, they finally found this group. The Church of the Nazarene officially accepted the group in 1988.

Nigeria's population has grown significantly since that World War II serviceman returned to his home country. Urbanization is rapid.

According to a United Nations (UN) report from July 2015, "Nigeria's population, currently the seventh largest in the world, is growing the most rapidly. Consequently, the population of Nigeria is projected to surpass that of the United States by about 2050, at which point it would become the third largest country in the world."

In 2015, Abuja, the nation's capital, was estimated to have a population of 2.44 million in an area of 356,668 square miles (574,100 square kilometers). In other words, Abuja has almost three times the population of Indianapolis, Indiana, USA living in an area that is (slightly) smaller! It is growing quickly, and poverty has increased. According to the UN, Lagos's (LAY-gaws) population is growing at 9.4 percent, and satellite areas around Abuja are growing at 20–30 percent. Meanwhile rapidly increasing rates of poverty are leaving 58 percent of the urban population living below US $1 per day.

Although 512 languages are spoken in Nigeria, in Abuja, the main languages are English, Hausa (HOU-sah), Ibo (EE-boh), and Yoruba (yoh-REW-bah). The Church of the Nazarene has worked primarily with one people group, the Efik (EF-fik), in the Abak (AH-bak) Akwa Ibom (AH-kwah EE-Bahm) area tucked in the southeast corner of the country.

A Kindled Heart and Mind

David Okon (OH-kahn) is a Nigerian who attended Africa Nazarene University from 2006 to 2009. One of his professors, Dr. Daryll Stanton, assigned a class project; students were to write about the history and the origin of the Church of the Nazarene in their home districts.

David discovered that although the Church of the Nazarene had been in Nigeria for decades, the church did not have a presence in the cities. God lit a passion in his heart that everybody in all social classes and tribes need to hear the message of holiness.

After he returned to Nigeria, when he was on a trip, Okon's car broke down in Abuja. He called a friend to help him. As they talked, David told his friend about his vision that the holiness message would be preached in Abuja through the Church of the Nazarene.

David told the district superintendent that he was ready to go plant a church in the capital. The district prayed for him and raised funds for his transportation.

He went to the suburb called Mararaba (mah-rah-RAH-ba), the most populated town in Abuja Outstate for new beginners (a place where new people to Abuja stay before moving to the central area). He reached out to people and found some Nazarenes who had migrated to Abuja. However, many of them had already moved on to another church or religious path.

Abuja has a religious population that can be unsympathetic to Christianity. Because of this, the congregation has faced difficulties. David states, "God is really faithful to us and *He* continues to add to His body as we reach out to the people."

While he is trying to tell others about Jesus, Pastor Okon has been told that people come to Abuja to find employment—not a church. He says, "As we listened to people and their need, I had the vision of establishing urban agriculture so that most of the members would work and earn a living until they may finally get government work."

He has started to make that vision a reality.

The communities lease a small parcel of land, which they will cultivate for five years. He hopes that as the idea grows, the parcels of land available will also expand. By feeding the stomach and enabling people to have the dignity of work, he hopes to reach more souls for Christ.

*He said to them, "Go into all the world and preach the gospel to all creation.
Whoever believes and is baptized will be saved, but whoever does not believe will be condemned.
And these signs will accompany those who believe:
In my name they will drive out demons;
they will speak in new tongues;
they will pick up snakes with their hands;
and when they drink deadly poison,
it will not hurt them at all;
they will place their hands on sick people,
and they will get well."*
—Mark 16:15-18

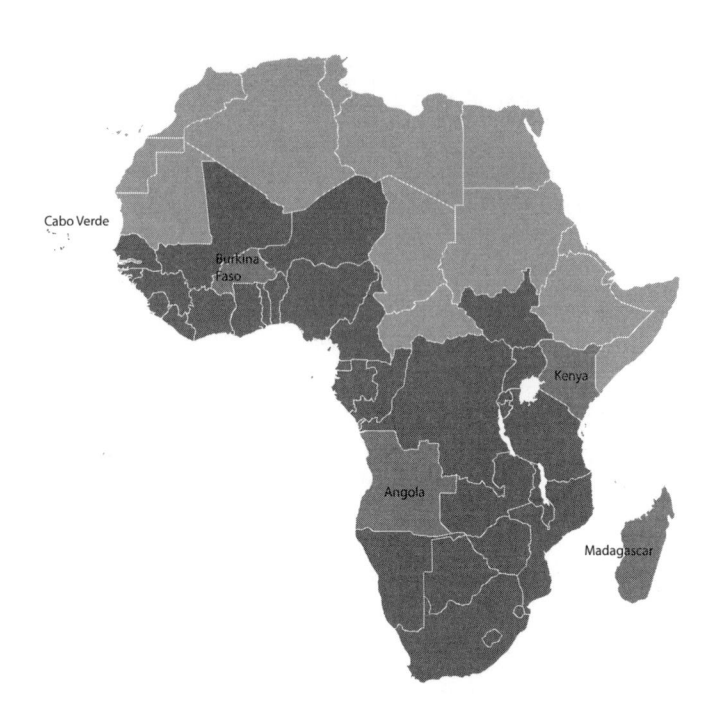

Cabo Verde

Burkina Faso

Kenya

Angola

Madagascar

Chapter 5
PARTNERS AND LEADERS

A single finger can't lift meat from the plate.
—Cameroon (kah-mer-OON) proverb

Imagine a sermon ending with an hour-long altar call.

And then people wouldn't return to their seats. So a second sermon was preached to people who seemed to thirst for more and more of God's Word.

The spiritual hunger of the Nazarenes is one evidence of how God is moving in Angola and throughout Africa.

Partners for the Mission

Danilo and Maria Carvalho (kah-VI-yoh), Cabo Verdeans, spent 16 years pastoring and helping establish the Church of the Nazarene in Portugal. After Danilo worked on a master's degree at Nazarene Theological College in Manchester, England, the Carvalhos returned to the Africa Region.

In 2008, they were sent to Angola to teach, plant churches, counsel, train leaders, and coordinate construction projects. Maria also trains women and children for ministry.

Angola is the second-largest diamond- and oil-producing country in Sub-Saharan Africa, yet its people are among Africa's poorest. Even though many Nazarenes in Angola live in poverty, they have generously given to mission causes. As a Xisonga (ki-SON-gah) proverb states: "Children who are siblings share the head of a locust," which means in a family, family members are willing to sacrifice for others.

The ties between the Carvalhos' home country and their assigned country are deepening.

The lengthy Angolan Civil War (1975–2002) disrupted the education of hundreds of thousands of school-age children. A family in Cabo Verde donated money to build a school—Escola (esk-OH-la) Nazarena Engenhiero (en-jen-YER-oh) Samuel Monteiro—in Lubango (lew-BAHN-goh), one of Angola's largest cities.

The government has recognized the school. This means the fees can be lowered and the ministry of the school, which currently serves 300 students, can be expanded. The building is multifunctional—a primary school during the day, a school for adults during the evenings, and a youth center during holidays.

People are hungry to learn about regular school subjects, but also about spiritual things.

A few years ago, a pastor's conference, originally planned to teach evangelism and discipleship strategies, turned into a revival.

"As I began to teach, I recognized that the questions asked were not related to how to evangelize and make disciples," Filimao Chambo explains. "There was a much deeper hunger and thirst for the righteousness of God. I had to put my notes aside and answer the questions about holiness lifestyle. The focus became biblical holiness and every single teaching session and service turned into a time for people to meet God."

Dr. Chambo, Dr. Paulo Sueia (se-WAY-ah), and Danilo prayed with people at the altars. Prayer times were extended as leaders reconciled with one another. Conferees made renewed commitments to preaching, holy living, and God. Children and youth turned to God for forgiveness of their sins and to be filled with the Spirit of the Lord. Wonderful testimonies celebrated how the Lord had sanctified the people. The leaders were encouraged and looking forward to going back to their home areas to teach and preach the message of holiness.

Dr. Chambo recalls the final morning, "People literally ran to the altar crying out to the Lord to be filled with the Holy Spirit. The prayer time went on for over an hour. When we finally asked people to return to their seats, no one moved. So, I preached again and then we prayed again. Young and old testified that the Lord sanctified them. The Lord visited us in a way I have never seen before in my life."

Danilo says, "Being missionaries in Angola is something we do with love, fear, and deep conviction of God's call. God is on His throne in Angola!"

Growing Leadership Potential

Missionary Mary Ganda was a children's Sunday School teacher when she felt a call to reach beyond her own village and to share the gospel in other ethnic groups and countries. Life moved on and Mary married Friday Ganda... but as they built their home together, she still felt the draw to work in other places. She admitted this to Friday and learned that God had also called him. Now they work together.

Friday had been saved in 1986 when a friend had shared the gospel. Friday joined the Church of the Nazarene in 1988. Two years later, he enrolled at Kenya Nazarene Bible College (now Nazarene Bible College of East Africa in Nairobi). But in 1993, he went a step further in his spiritual life. "I surrendered my whole life for the Lord to take full charge," he said. And the Lord did! Friday rejoiced in his sanctification.

After Bible college, Friday and Mary accepted a pastoral call to a town near Lake Victoria in Kenya. The church grew; soon he was elected as superintendent of the Kenya Southwest District (now Kenya Lake Victoria District). The district grew too, and Friday sensed God calling him to go beyond his own culture.

About that time, Friday wrote, "We need to understand that we are born into a new family. This is a family, comprised of people from different earthly tribes. This is a family headed by one Father. We no longer answer to this world, nor do we belong to this earthly tribe, but to the Lord God our Father."

The next step for Friday was to serve as the JESUS Film coordinator for East and Central Africa, which included six countries. Later, the Gandas would be appointed to the Horn of Africa.

Friday states, "My vision has been to preach the gospel of holiness to unreached people, identify with the upcoming and called leaders, nurture them to [reach] various fields of ministry as they feel called."

When Mary and Friday Ganda enter a new area, they do so with the end in mind. They systematically work themselves out of a job by training leaders. They trust God to provide a next step, and He always has. After ministering in the Horn of Africa, they served in Burkina Faso.

Mary & Friday Ganda

Friday remembered early days in Burkina Faso, when he asked God to give him the right person for this country. He says, "I was keenly aware that God never let us down."

The day his mentee, Rev. Joseph Tiendrebeogo (tee-en-DRAY-bay-oh-goh), was named as the district superintendent, Friday said, "Today I praised the Lord as I said, 'Thank you, God, for fulfilling your promise.'"

In his book, *Practical Leadership: Passing the Baton*, Friday writes:

> Though culture and languages differ, and circumstances change, God's purpose for His people does not change.
>
> We can raise them (leaders) in a very short time, let them loose to take over from us and be ready to move to newer areas where we do not have churches.

Finally, I help them understand that Christ is passing the baton when He says to "Go into all the world." This means everybody is called.

A Continuing Impact

Ronald Miller currently serves as the regional NYI coordinator for Africa. Previously, he and his wife, Shelly, served as missionaries on the African island nation of Madagascar.

Ronald was exposed to many missionaries while he was growing up in South Africa. As a young adult, he served on the Nazarene Impact Team, which traveled from country to country within the African continent, to share the gospel. Ronald was a team member in 1995. The next two years he served as the team leader. He also helped coordinate teams for several years.

When Ronald Miller arrived in Madagascar as a missionary, he naturally introduced the concept of Impact Teams as a way to evangelize. Impact Teams, ministry outside the local church, and some of Ronald's other visions were new to Madagascar. The leadership grabbed the idea, and training began.

"We were praying for 14 dedicated people to comprise the team, knowing that not all who trained would follow through with the projects," Ronald says. "When training started, more than 30 people responded to the call. This was truly exciting."

The leadership set a goal that each church in the district would train and equip a mini-Impact Team each year. One church with a mini-Impact team held a Vacation

Bible School through which 200 children gave their lives to Christ.

Because of Impact Team training, each person on the team is able to assist the local church leaders, pray powerfully, and bring each child and the families they represent to the feet of the Lord. Malagasy (mah-lah-GAHS-ee) leaders are hopeful and prayerful about the future ministry of these teams.

Tarryn Jody Nathan, a ministerial student from Nazarene Theological College in South Africa, went to Madagascar as part of a RSA Gauteng (HOU-tayng) District Work & Witness trip. She writes that on the second morning, "We had orientation with the missionary Ronald Miller. Then we were introduced to the evangelism team—mostly teenagers between the ages of 14 and 17—that we worked with for 13 days. We started with door-to-door outreach, sharing the gospel through the evangelism bracelet [a bracelet with different colored portions that help the wearers explain the gospel based on the color schemes] and the EvangeCube [a cube of picture sections that can be manipulated different ways to explain a gospel presentation]. That evening, more than 100 children and adults accepted Jesus as their personal Lord and Savior after seeing the JESUS Film."

The team is always on call to help local churches. For instance, one pastor was already working with a church that was about a year old, but decided to plant another church farther away. She asked the evangelism team to be a part of the first Sunday gathering at her new church—she knew the presence of the team could lend excitement and result in people quickly spreading the word about the team through a community. And in turn, the team helped through singing, drama, and just talking to people.

Ronald Miller has multiplied himself. He instilled the training he received into others' lives. As a result, he has made an eternal impact on all those who meet the Madagascar evangelism teams.

Ronald Miller

Filimao Chambo is proud of the Millers and all of the members of the Africa team, no matter what their areas of responsibility. "The Church of the Nazarene in Africa has always been committed to missionary work. There are several leaders from Africa who have served and others who continue to serve as missionaries, deployed by the Global Church and/or the Africa Region as global missionaries, volunteers, regional missionaries, and specialized assignment," he says. "The impact they have made, and the impact others continue to make in our Bible colleges, fields, countries, regional office, is applauded."

*Declare his glory among the nations,
his marvelous deeds among all peoples.*
—1 Chronicles 16:24

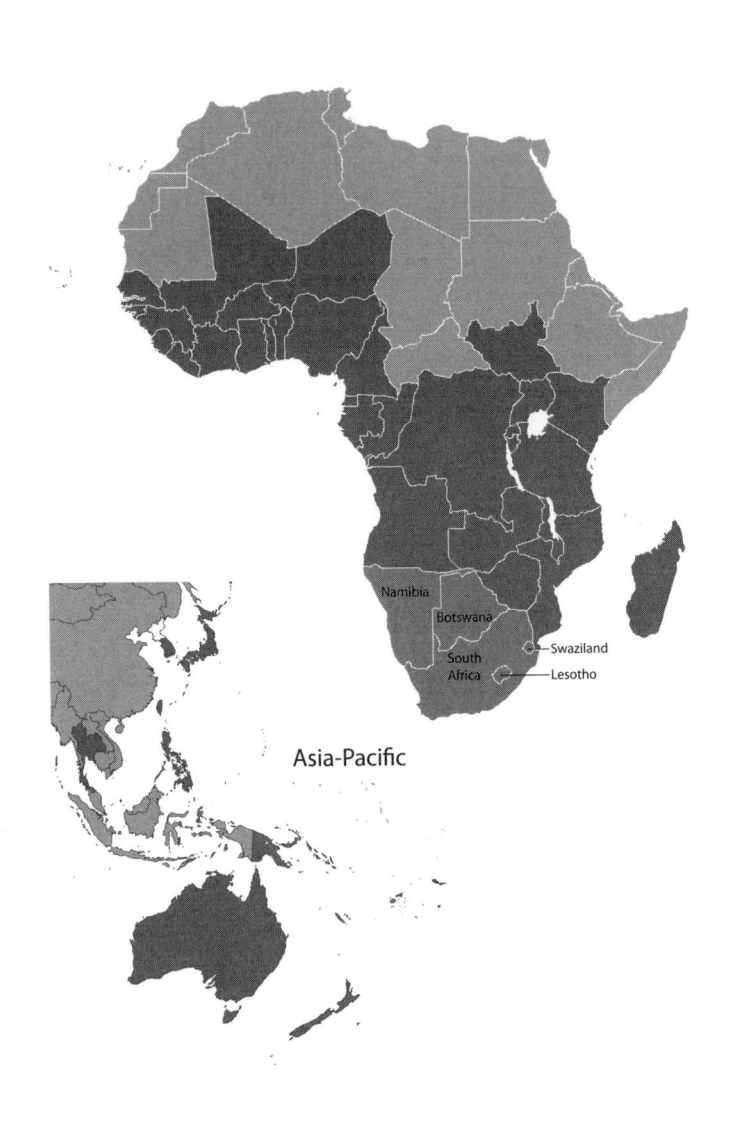

Namibia
Botswana
Swaziland
South Africa
Lesotho

Asia-Pacific

Chapter 6
HOLINESS IS LOVE IN ACTION

A dish that is going to be tasty smells good when it boils.
—Senegal proverb

While African missionaries have reached other countries within their own region for years, the Africa Region is now celebrating the sending of South Africans Collin and Shireen (sher-REEN) Elliott to the Asia-Pacific Region as Africa's first global missionaries. The Elliotts expertly express encouragement and love for children, congregations, coworkers, and more. They are wonderful messengers of holiness.

The Miracle

Collin Elliott's childhood experience reminds him of the great impact that showing love to a child can have.

Collin's background includes being from a Hindu family in South Africa. At three years old, he could not walk, and

Author's note: From the Africa Regional Office, the Elliots are not the first missionaries to be sent from Africa, but they are the first African missionaries on a global contract to serve in another region.

his father almost gave him up for adoption to an uncle and aunt who did not have a male child. His mother, a Christian, prayed for a miracle—that he would be healed. She also prayed that the Lord would block the adoption to an ardent Hindu family.

God answered those prayers and the whole family rejoiced when three-year-old Collin started walking. He still walks in the "light of Jesus" physically and spiritually. He says he is thankful that the Lord stepped in and that he is not a Hindu priest but a pastor on behalf of the great Shepherd, Jesus, who is the Christ.

Apartheid was the rule in South Africa when Collin was young. He clearly remembers that, when he was four years old, he and his family were put into dumpsters by the apartheid government and relocated to a township called Chatsworth. Wherever he testifies, he mentions that he "came on a dumpster to be a discipler for Jesus Christ."

When he was six years old, he noticed a group of white people down the road. He and his friends, a gang in the making, went to harass the group of people they had been taught to hate. But this group was a work team—a precursor to Work & Witness teams. The team loved and embraced the boys.

Though he may have pretended to visit the team each day to see their construction progress, the real reason he returned every day was to experience more of the love they showed to him through giving him hugs and candy. He was saved at the age of six and involved and trained in the church ever since.

"Everybody can embrace children and say, I love you," Collin encourages. "We need to touch young lives."

Shireen has a special burden to equip children for ministry. She feels reaching children is a Christlike act because Jesus blessed them and said, "Let the little children come to me, and do not hinder them, for the kingdom of heaven belongs to such as these" (Matthew 19:14). She feels children must be accepted, loved, valued, and respected.

She wrote:

> The 4-14-year-old [age groups] ministry in the Church is vital in fulfilling the Great Commission. This age group can pray, sing, and lead a worship service. They can invite their friends to services and be involved in ministry. They need to be incorporated into the ministry of the church. Children should feel part of, and know they belong to, their church. They should be taken into membership as soon as they acknowledge Jesus Christ as Lord and have chosen to accept Him into their hearts and be a disciple and follower of Jesus Christ. They should also be given responsibilities in the Kingdom as soon as they understand their faith in Jesus Christ.
>
> Our churches can flourish and grow when we see the importance of ministry to children. We need to reach the lost children, rescue children from oppression, root our children in Christ, the Author and Finisher of our faith, and release them to reap the harvest of souls.

A team from Bethany (Oklahoma, USA) First Church of the Nazarene was ministering in Swaziland, and Collin and Shireen were traveling with the group for a few days. At the last minute, the person who was to speak to a primary school assembly had to cancel. Shireen stepped in and held the large sanctuary of children enraptured.

She began with this story:

> A six-year-old boy went fishing with live worms. He put the worm on the hook and caught a fish to eat.
>
> Later when he was at school, he was asked, "How can you say Jesus lives in your heart?"
>
> He explained it was like fishing. He can't see the fish or hear the fish; but when it tugs on the line, he knows that it is there.
>
> "Jesus tugs on the line of my heart," he said.
>
> When we accept Jesus, He comes in and wants to cleanse us. When He cleanses us, He fills us with himself and then uses us to tell others about Him so they can receive Jesus in their hearts and have eternal life. We are not to keep this message a secret, but to spread it to everyone.

Shireen believes in hugging children, saying that it is the most important time in a person's life to feel valued. And children respond to Collin and Shireen's love and belief in their potential for the Kingdom.

Encouraging and Equipping Coworkers

Collin and Shireen began their ministry adventure when they met at Nazarene Theological College in Port Elizabeth, South Africa (now Nazarene Theological College—in Honeydew, South Africa [serving the South Field]), earning their diplomas in theology. Both are ordained elders who model what they want to see in their coworkers. They are passionate about winning souls to Christ, making disciples, planting churches, and education.

Beginning in 2000, Collin served as the Africa South Field strategy coordinator, which included overseeing the Church of the Nazarene in South Africa, Swaziland, Lesotho (loo-SOO-too), Namibia, and Botswana. The Elliotts' responsibilities included vision casting, spiritual strategy and skills formation, administration, missionary care, volunteer missionary service, overseeing all institutions on the field, and compassionate ministry.

Shireen & Collin Elliott

They organized annual training conferences to equip district superintendents and pastors to effectively strategize so they can meet mission objectives. During Collin

Elliott's years as Africa South Field strategy coordinator, field membership grew by more than 100 percent.

"I thank God for His favor and presence and for a good field team to continue strategies for multiplication and spiritual health and growth," Elliott said.

In 2009, Collin earned a Master of Theology in Christian counseling. He and Shireen were commissioned as global missionaries in the Church of the Nazarene in 2010. Collin and Shireen's work as role models and encouragers expanded to the entire region when the regional director, Filimao Chambo, appointed Collin as assistant to the regional director for Church Growth and District Development in 2012.

When Collin was still field strategy coordinator, Shireen was given her own new task. She was asked to lead a project to plant new churches in the major cities on the Africa South Field, Shireen responded with excitement and a prayer request for God's wisdom.

She pastored the Shallcross (SHAHL-craws) Church of the Nazarene (RSA Kwa Zulu Natal District) near Durban, South Africa, for two years. Her goal is not to teach people to follow legalistic rules, but to disciple them so they can listen to the Spirit's internal voice for guidance.

The church grew from 207 to 484 under Shireen's leadership and was instrumental in planting two other churches and establishing a new preaching point. One church started as self-supporting and the other was also strong, as Shireen empowered lay people.

Shireen also has a gift for organization. This has been obvious as she has put together large events for the region. Her task may be getting all the delegates and visitors to general assemblies and making sure they were cared for or helping with a woman's extravaganza or woman's clergy conference. Her last highly successful event was the 2015 Africa Regional Conference in Johannesburg, which occurred even as the Elliotts were planning a move to the Asia-Pacific Region.

Collin and Shireen are hospitable. They believe in listening to people's dreams and hopes. They take an interest in each individual, even in groups as large as Work & Witness teams. Conversations go long around their table. Teams have left the Africa South Field feeling like family, not strangers, thanks in a great degree to the Elliotts' effort to love and encourage.

You did not choose me, but I chose you and appointed you so that you might go and bear fruit—fruit that will last— and so that whatever you ask in my name the Father will give you.
—John 15:16

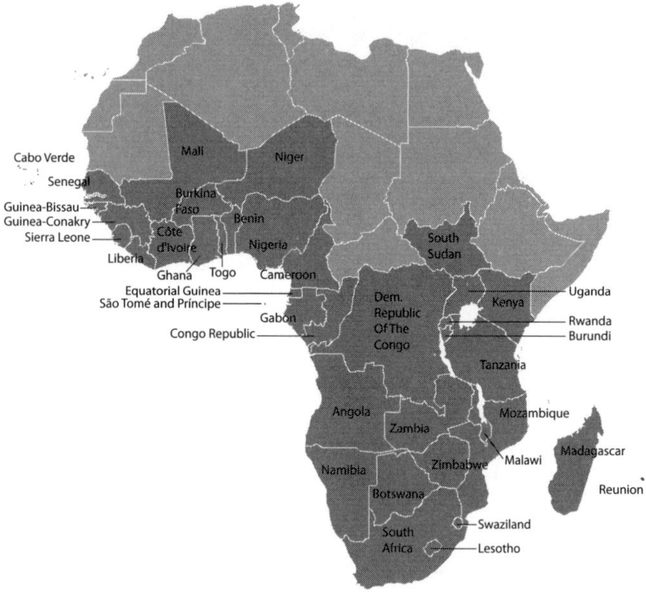
Cabo Verde
Senegal
Guinea-Bissau
Guinea-Conakry
Sierra Leone
Liberia
Mali
Niger
Burkina Faso
Côte d'Ivoire
Ghana
Togo
Benin
Nigeria
Cameroon
Equatorial Guinea
São Tomé and Príncipe
Gabon
Congo Republic
South Sudan
Dem. Republic Of The Congo
Uganda
Kenya
Rwanda
Burundi
Tanzania
Angola
Zambia
Mozambique
Malawi
Madagascar
Reunion
Namibia
Zimbabwe
Botswana
South Africa
Swaziland
Lesotho

Chapter 7
A PLACE OF RESPONSIBILITY

If your brother crosses the river, hold the rope.
—Burundi proverb

"Love is no exception, even though the substance of it does not change from culture to culture, the circumstances differ. How love is expressed is very much culturally conditioned." —Gift Mtukwa (m-TEWK-wah), religion faculty at Africa Nazarene University, Kenya.

General Superintendent Eugénio Duarte noted at the Elliotts' sending service in Johannesburg that they were not called to a place of privilege, but a place of responsibility.

Not only are the missionaries called to a new level of responsibility, but so are the sending and receiving churches—and all are accepting this responsibility with both hands. As we can see, the Church of the Nazarene in Africa and Asia-Pacific will hold the rope as the Elliotts cross the water.

Expressing Holiness Through Love

A main challenge Collin and Shireen Elliott face is to learn how to express holiness through love in other cultures.

Collin is looking forward to making a difference. He says, "That's all you need to do, touch lives. When you touch a life, the impact lasts for all eternity."

In a goodbye note sent to their coworkers in Africa, Collin wrote:

> Our resolve is always to spread the full gospel of salvation in the provision and hope we possess in our resurrected Lord and Savior Jesus Christ. As we float and resonate in this cloud of hope, the milk of human compassion must never go sour in our Christlike service to all mankind. We will serve in a region other than our own with diverse cultures, customs, languages, and people groups, but it has dawned upon us that our responsibility is to "make Christlike disciples in the nations," not by being alike but being in love.
>
> We feel like the pilot on his first solo plane voyage when he said, "The worst is not to fail, but not dare to try." We understand that the "future is as bright as the promises of God" [Adoniram Judson]. Just thinking about that statement, I did something that I never did before; I bought myself a pair of sunglasses.

Collin says, "Africans understand they can do things for themselves and even beyond. We have to think as a family and a team—not 'us' and 'them' language which creates barriers." We are an international church family that can share the work of spreading the message of holiness in new and creative ways.

The Sending Church

The Elliotts' commissioning service at the Africa Regional Conference in 2015 was opened by Jackie Joseph, NMI coordinator for the Africa Region. After prayer, Rev. Joseph announced the goals for the year, which included sending missionaries from Africa to Africa and around the world and establishing the church in two major cities where the church has a limited presence.

"It is a day of celebration for Africa to send a missionary to another region," said Africa East Field Strategy Coordinator Don Gardner, who spoke on behalf of all the region's field strategy coordinators. He added, "You have left your footprints all over Africa."

General Superintendent Eugénio Duarte stated, "We are giving some of our best to the rest of the world. I am proud of the Africa Region. A church that has received some of the best that have come from America and Europe has learned to do the same—to send some of our best."

The regional commissioning service was not the only goodbye. As soon as the announcement about this missions deployment was made, churches from the Africa South Field wanted to express their appreciation for Collin and Shireen. The Morka (MOOR-kah) Church of the Nazarene hosted a service two weeks before the Elliotts left the Region. Pastor Tim and Mrs. Tembi Mogorosi (TEM-bee moh-goh-ROH-see) invited those from nearby churches to join them as an encouragement for the Elliotts. Together they praised the Lord and prayed for the days ahead.

Rev. Mashangu Maluleka (mah-SHAN-gew mah-lew-LAY-kah), strategy coordinator for the Africa South Field, reminded the crowd that "When God calls missionaries, he is also calling the church to support them in prayer and finances."

The Receiving Church

The Asia-Pacific Region has welcomed the arrival of Collin and Shireen Elliott as team members.

Regional Director Mark Louw says, "Their coming has been an answer to prayer and a source of great anticipation on my part. Collin and Shireen epitomize servant leadership and have come to the Region from Africa with servant hearts. They are coming to learn and serve, listen and share, encourage and be encouraged, challenge thinking and be challenged by reality. In brief, they're here to be contributing members of the team."

Collin serves the Asia-Pacific Region as the New Initiatives coordinator (Church Planting, Evangelism, and Church Growth). He plans to take the Church in creative ways to where it is not yet, and Shireen is Women's Clergy coordinator, focusing on empowering and developing women in and for ministry.

*While they were worshiping the Lord and fasting,
the Holy Spirit said,
"Set apart for me Barnabas and Saul for the work
to which I have called them."
So after they had fasted and prayed,
they placed their hands on them and sent them off.*
—Acts 13:2–3

Sub-Saharan African

South Africa

Chapter 8
THE FUTURE OF MISSIONS IN AFRICA

A container is filled little by little.
—Kenya proverb

The Church in Africa has seen great growth through the efforts of missionaries and local congregations, but much remains to be done. The future of missions in Africa presents continuing challenges. A lot of these stem from demographic trends on the continent.

New Challenges, New Opportunities

Africa's population is growing at an extraordinary rate. Since 1996, the countries of Sub-Saharan Africa have had the highest annual population growth rate of any region, according to data from the World Bank (http://data.worldbank.org). While most regions' annual population growth rate has decreased gradually since 1964, Sub-Saharan Africa's has *increased*.

Much of Africa's population growth has been in urban areas. In 1964, fewer than one in six people in Sub-Saharan Africa lived in urban areas. By 2014, more than one in three lived there. If that change doesn't seem like a dramatic difference, consider the raw numbers. In 1964 fewer than 40 million Africans lived in cities; by 2014, more than 357 million did!

While the population of Sub-Saharan Africa has increased, more Sub-Saharan Africans have pursued higher education than ever before. African people of university age in 2014 were more than five times more likely than those in 1974 to be enrolled in universities or other institutions of higher education.

These demographic trends present new challenges and new opportunities for missions in Africa. Two key areas where work is already underway are university ministries and urban ministries.

University Ministries

The work of Rev. Mashangu Maluleka at the Tshwane (SHWAH-nee) University of Technology shows the kind of impact that university ministry can have in Africa. Mashangu had a vision for a Church of the Nazarene to be part of this university, located in Pretoria, South Africa.

More than eight years ago, a few students registered a student organization that has grown into the Divine Hope Church of the Nazarene. Sunday School is held in lecture halls. Students ask questions and participate in the discussion. Bibles are open and laughter is commonly heard.

Church is held in a large auditorium. As they enter, people are greeted with a hug and a smile. The service is seamlessly led by musicians and other leaders as more than

200 people gather to praise God. Every service is videotaped and available for those who miss a week or want to share a service with others.

This church offers more than a Sunday morning service. Fourteen small groups meet throughout the week. There is a midweek service. The people actively participate in RSA Gauteng District events. The community is strong.

After the service, newcomers are invited to share juice and a snack. They are personally welcomed to become a part of Divine Hope by Mashangu and Remember Maluleka, who explain that they do not expect students to transfer their membership from their home church, but to see Divine Hope as a place to encounter God while at the university.

Special events related to the university also dot the calendar. The church participates in New Student Orientation and welcomes students when they first arrive. They also have a major emphasis on praying for students who are sitting for exams. Two thousand students once attended a three-hour prayer meeting for exams.

Mashangu's vision is not for this church alone, but for every secular university in South Africa to have its own Divine Hope Church of the Nazarene. This is a big vision, but God gives, and fulfills, big visions!

Urban Ministries

In many African countries, cities are growing rapidly. Sometimes this growth brings problems like gangs, drugs, theft, shootings, and more. The challenges are great, but so are the opportunities. Both new and established churches have the chance to reach large numbers of people through activities and programs.

The townships of Bonteheuwel (bon-te-YAH-voh) and Valhalla Park in Cape Town, South Africa, experienced problems due to gangs in 2013. Local Nazarene pastors worked with community leaders to offer a safe space and programs for a weekend. Activities included an outdoor concert for youth, free blood pressure checks, programs for children, the distribution of reading glasses, and a 50th anniversary worship service for the church's district, RSA Western Cape.

"The Holy Spirit moved in the hearts and lives of hundreds of children, youth, and adults. Part of each activity was dedicated to one-on-one prayer and counseling. During these times many surrendered their lives to Christ," missionary Jodi Cooper reported in the *Out of Africa* newsletter.

The difficulties of urbanization can be daunting. But, when people are hurting, the Church has the responsibility and the privilege to show them—not just tell them about—the love of Jesus.

This demonstration of love may take the form of providing safe spaces in a dangerous environment. It may look like providing job training in an area where high joblessness discourages youth and pushes them towards drugs, alcohol, gangs, or other problematic activities. It may entail providing health services or educational opportunities. In all cases, though, for people to see real and lasting transformation in their lives and communities they will need an invitation to begin a relationship with Jesus.

The future of the Church in Africa will involve intentional interactions with people in cities. As Mashangu Maluleka says, "African big cities, we are coming."

Qualifying the Called

A favorite saying of ours is that God doesn't call the qualified; He qualifies the called. As God calls Africans to missionary work in Africa and beyond, the region is working to equip them.

"For many years, missions was done by outsiders coming to Africa, so now we want to provide the same opportunities for those God is calling from Africa to be able to go and serve," says David Cooper, the Africa Region Mobilization and Personnel coordinator.

One of the ways they are being equipped is through events called Nazarene Missions Orientation. These two-day workshops help participants "learn about the Church's approach to missions and discuss how to effectively minister in other cultures," according to a report from one of the orientations. Some workshops focus on groups preparing for short-term mission trips while others are geared towards young people who feel a call for mission work.

Stephen Phillips, a project coordinator for Nazarene Compassionate Ministries—Africa, has attended several orientations and says it changed his view of a missionary from "someone who has money" and "someone from the USA" to "someone who has been called by God and sent out by his or her local church."

"The first M.O. [Missions Orientation] I attended changed my view of missions. I don't believe that I fully understood what it means to be part of a global church. This was the big mindset change," Stephen adds.

Beyond the efforts to train people in missions, the region has a bigger focus to develop a missiology for Africa. It is important to have a theology of missions that "is consistent with our context, a missiology that is consistent with our realities in Africa, while at the same time, is consistent with our Global Church identity and missionary vision," says Dr. Chambo.

As leaders continue to develop this missiology, God continues to call Africans, and many are answering.

"If God has sent you, do you think He cares if the network reaches there? There is someone He wants to reach in that community.... God continues to invite His church to be a part of His mission," says Filimao Chambo.

Again Jesus said, "Peace be with you!
As the Father has sent me, I am sending you."
—John 20:21

CONCLUSION

*The sleep that lasts from one market day
to the next becomes death.*
—Nigeria proverb

The proverb reminds us that we need to take action. Africa South Field Strategy Coordinator Mashangu Maluleka notes, "As far as the mission of God is involved, we have no choice. If we are not a church involved in missions, we are not a church."

Rev. Samantha Chambo wrote, "Africans default to community. I have seen the power of this truth displayed in various ways as believers take ownership of events and projects and run with them. There will be an explosion of Christlike disciples on the continent if every believer believes that they are called and empowered to be active participants in the mission of Christ."

In the realm of missions, we can all have a part in reaching the world for Jesus. Let's look at some of the ways we can do this.

Pray and Encourage

When talking with visitors to South Africa, Collin Elliott related the impact a small church had. The church sent notes to encourage him and Shireen through difficult days. He added, "When a church remembers its missionaries and sends cards faithfully, they are a large church. They are praying for us and for the ministry we do. They are a big church involved in the big ways that our big God is moving." He stresses that nobody can do things all alone. We need to partner and stay connected with each other.

Others may choose to encourage missionaries through social media.

If you want to create a system to pray for the missionaries, you might want to start by making a list of the missionaries mentioned in this book. Or you can see profiles of more missionaries at www.nazarene.org/MissionaryProfiles.

To keep up with mission prayer needs, sign up for the NMI Prayer Mobilization Line (PML) or read it on the NMI webpage: www.nazarenemissions.org. You can also "like" PML on Facebook to get the latest requests from around the world.

Give and Send

Ezekiel Mnisi (m-NEE-see), Africa's representative on the Global NMI Council, said, "We tend to think we have ownership. 'This is my house.' 'This is my car.' But it is true that we don't have anything. What we think we have is what God has entrusted to us. When He wants us to use it, He expects obedience from us."

He reminded the workshop attendees at the Regional Conference in Nairobi that when raising funds for mission projects, "The ultimate goal is not money, it is souls."

We need to give with the right attitude. Mashangu Maluleka reminds us. "Obedience is better than sacrifice."

Go and Spread the Message of Holiness

Enoch Litswele said, "The good news reached you and me because someone obeyed and came to tell us about Jesus Christ. After we were saved from our sins, we also became part of the commissioned."

After hearing someone say that it is now Africa's turn for leading in the mission enterprise, Mashangu said, "Not 'it is Africa's turn,' but rather, 'Come, let's go.'" Africa is willing to partner with the greater church, but unwilling to have others give up or stop answering God's call for their lives in order to let Africa lead the way.

Enoch agrees, saying, "The fact that 'we are coworkers together' will be seen in our cooperative efforts to reach the world with the Good News and teach all people everything Jesus Christ has commanded us."

The Africa regional website (www.africanazarene.org) states that we have "the resolve to equip and empower every African Nazarene for service, first to their own people group, and then for cross-cultural ministry."

Let us not let any Nazarene child from this day forward feel as Samantha Chambo did when she wrote, "It was later in life that I realized it took more than a call on your life to be a missionary. I learned in my church that missionaries are normally 'white people' who were sent by the whole Church to share the Good News to Africans. My missionary dreams faded into the background."

Let us partner with the missionaries whom God has called from Africa and all other regions. Let us see beyond backgrounds to focus on our common mission as messengers of holiness.

Filimao Chambo challenges the Church, "In the same way people came to us saying the light is here, we don't need to live in darkness. God calls us to go and prepare the way of the Lord."

A voice of one calling:
*"In the wilderness prepare the way for the L*ORD*;*
make straight in the desert a highway for our God.
Every valley shall be raised up,
every mountain and hill made low;
the rough ground shall become level,
the rugged places a plain.
*And the glory of the L*ORD *will be revealed,*
and all people will see it together.
*For the mouth of the L*ORD *has spoken."*
—Isaiah 40:3-5

ACT ON IT

- As an individual, what cross-cultural concepts from this book do you believe need to be incorporated into your life? Ask God to enable to help you do that, then share them with a small group (Sunday School class, church board, Bible study, or prayer group) or other individuals.

- Small churches (or NMI small groups) might want to read the book during a specific timeframe and use it as a book club discussion or a mission education lesson, relating the discussion to your local congregation.

- Social media allows any reader to be personally connected, which encourages specific praying and giving. How can you—as an individual, small group, or congregation—use social media to connect to missionaries or Nazarenes around the world?

- Your participation in the World Evangelism Fund provides opportunity for missionaries, such as the ones in this book, to minister. The funds may be used directly for salary or indirectly to keep schools and districts operational. Pray about your level of participation in the World Evangelism Fund, and ask God to give direction for further participation.

- More than anything, pray for the people in this book or for people like them. Intercede for Nazarene missionaries, district and local church leaders around the world, and the members of thousands of global Nazarene congregations.